Name: _____

Date: _____

Location: _____

Notes:

Looking In From the Outside

Creating Your Own Window
A PERSONAL DEVELOPMENT WORKBOOK

Troy H. Seidl, Ph.D.

Outskirts Press, Inc.
Denver, Colorado

The opinions expressed in this manuscript are solely the opinions of the author and do not represent the opinions or thoughts of the publisher. The author has represented and warranted full ownership and/or legal right to publish all the materials in this book.

Looking In From The Outside
Creating Your Own Window
All Rights Reserved.
Copyright © 2011 Troy H. Seidl, Ph.D.
V3.0

Cover Photo Pixmac

This book may not be reproduced, transmitted, or stored in whole or in part by any means, including graphic, electronic, or mechanical without the express written consent of the publisher except in the case of brief quotations embodied in critical articles and reviews.

Outskirts Press, Inc.
http://www.outskirtspress.com

ISBN: 978-1-4327-5833-2

Outskirts Press and the "OP" logo are trademarks belonging to Outskirts Press, Inc.

PRINTED IN THE UNITED STATES OF AMERICA

Contents

Introduction	1
Pre-Test	9
My Life Story	11
Your Mode (M.O.D.E.)	25
The Best Fit	43
360 Degree Assessment	53
People You Know	67
Mental Stretching	77
Personal Development Plan	91
Post-Test	108
Final Thoughts	111

Introduction

Less than two weeks prior to the ill-fated Challenger blast-off in 1986, Florida Senator Bill Nelson was himself launched into outer space. This personal development workbook was inspired by the extraordinary life-changing moments he reveals about his journey. When sharing his experience with an audience or through his published book, *Mission, An American Congressman's Voyage to Space*, Senator Nelson explains in his own eloquent words, "…from space, it is abundantly clear that earth is very tiny and very precious. There are no dividing lines among countries. Seen from the perspective of space, political, racial, linguistic, and religious divisions disappear. Looking at earth from high up I saw only one globe – a planet that is itself a fragile spaceship in the black void of space. The thought kept running through my mind: if only all people could see earth as I could see it! Here floating in the midst of an airless blackness that stretches for billions of light years, is flung this fragile eco-system of a globe we call Earth."

Bill Nelson goes on to explain that "…it would be of tremendous value for political leaders to venture into space simply to witness earth from a truly global point of view. Maybe the next century a summit meeting will be held in space, where the leaders of the world, meeting to decide matters of war and peace, would experience for themselves the fragile unity of the earth in its lone journey." Perhaps the most telling part of Senator Nelson's experience is that, in his own words, "It was impossible to look out to earth, from this extraordinary perspective and remain unchanged."

It was this changing event, the view of earth that prompts the question, "How might a person create their own window so that s/he can look in from the outside?" In other words, can we gain the same kind of life-changing experience without traveling to space? The most striking part of Senator Nelson's experience was the simplistic nature of the events. All he had to do was peer through a shuttle window and suddenly his life was transformed. In the world of personal development, there are plenty of well-regarded comprehensive tools that are intended to help people develop themselves and better understand other people with whom they interact. However, it can and usually does take a great deal of time and commitment to clearly understand and utilize these personal tools. Consequently, it's not as simple as looking through a window. In fact, many of the most commonly used self-development tools are not always able to easily accommodate the fast-paced, technologically advancing world in which we currently live.

Looking in From the Outside, Creating Your Own Window is essentially the CliffsNotes for many of these complex instruments. This personal development workbook gives you the opportunity to experience a variety of development exercises without spending too much time, money, or effort in memorizing all kinds of codes, profiles, or sub-categories. Consequently, you will be able to utilize the activities in this book immediately as a way to develop yourself and better understand your experiences with the people around you. The idea is to enable you to spend your time using the tools in this book, rather than spending all your time figuring out *how* to use the tools. If you have a screwdriver with six buttons, multiple computer chips, an interchangeable handle, and a panic switch, and you also have a screwdriver with a solid handle but no extra buttons or switches, which tool would you rather use? Which tool would be easier to teach other people to use? Which tool would cost less time, money, and potential confusion? This workbook is your simple tool giving you an opportunity to work on your own personal development in a reasonable amount of time requiring only a reasonable amount of effort. Whether you are a successful executive with a great deal of experience, an emerging leader in a work setting, a student or a person who simply appreciates learning more about themselves, this workbook can and will prove beneficial.

The workbook is organized into seven activities. Each of the activities or exercises is based on some of the most popular and effective psychological and educational approaches that have been used for many years designed to foster individual and group development, both in work settings and in personal settings. As compared to some of the more complicated development tools, the instruments provided in this workbook are quicker to use, easier to understand and therefore more accommodating in this fast-paced busy world in which we live. Use a pen or pencil to complete each of the exercises. *You* are the actual author of this workbook, not someone else. Too often we rely on what an expert author or television pop psychologist tells us what to do and we have very little input in the matter. This is your chance to author your own change manual, making decisions that work well for you specifically. This will make more sense as you complete the exercises.

By following these simple and enjoyable activities, you will be able to create your own window, allowing you to gain a clearer perspective about yourself and about others. Most importantly, you have the chance to gain the life-changing, eye-opening views similar to what Senator Bill Nelson achieved during his journey through space.

"Most of the fundamental ideas of science are essentially simple, and may as a rule, be expressed in a language that is comprehensible to everyone."

-Albert Einstein

Before you get started, please complete this Pre-Test:

Rate the following statements according to the 5-point scale below. Circle the most appropriate number below each statement. Following the exercises in this workbook, you will be asked to complete the same set of ratings in a Post-Test.

1 = Strongly Disagree

2 = Disagree

3 = Neither Agree nor Disagree

4 = Agree

5 = Strongly Agree

1. I clearly understand myself.
   1   2   3   4   5

2. I clearly understand the people around me.
   1   2   3   4   5

3. I clearly understand why I behave the way I do.
   1   2   3   4   5

4. I clearly understand how my behavior affects other people.
   1   2   3   4   5

5. I clearly understand the needs of other people.
   1   2   3   4   5

6. I clearly understand how people perceive me.
   1   2   3   4   5

Activity One

My
Life Story

Happy Birthday! You are 100 years old. It is a time to celebrate your accomplishments. You must provide an autobiography of your life. In this first exercise, take some time to describe the story of your life. Always write in past tense as if you are 100 years old currently. In the study of psychology, there is power in reflection and this is a reflection of what you experienced in your life. Use the set of Writing Panels provided to describe all the things you can about your life.

Write your story from your childhood through adulthood, describing life after your retirement as well. What kind of work did you do? Where did you live? What goals did you achieve? Who were your friends? What did you study? Who did you meet? What were your accomplishments? When did you fail? When did you succeed? What was most important to you and what was least important to you? What did people think of you? What do you remember most? When did you retire? What did you do after retirement? Where did you live? What were significant events in your life? These are questions you can think about as you complete this first exercise, but don't limit yourself to only these questions. Write the story of *your* life. If you have a hard time knowing where to begin, just start writing and it will come to you. Make certain to cover your entire life in simple terms.

Don't get too caught up in one phase or stage of your life story. Try to fit your story into the five Writing Panels provided in the blank pages that follow.

My Life Story Writing Panel One

My Life Story Writing Panel Two

My Life Story Writing Panel Three

My Life Story Writing Panel Four

My Life Story Writing Panel Five

Questions

Answer the following questions using the space provided:

1. What about your Life Story struck you as most interesting?

2. What are you *most* proud of in your Life Story and why?

3. What are you *least* proud of in your Life Story and why?

4. What would you change about your Life Story and why?

5. How might reading your Life Story affect the decisions you make?

Conclusion

Consider your Life Story when you think about the decisions you make, the people you are drawn to, the kinds of desires you have and the things you avoid. Reflecting on your Life Story can provide a way for you to step back and consider what you are about to do or what decisions you are about to make and if they really fit into your life plan. The most unfortunate thing you can do is to never recognize your Life Story until your life has passed you by.

You are not limited to using this exercise as your only guide. The exercises in this workbook are all designed to complement this kind of perspective, whereby you gain a greater awareness about you and the world around you. Remember, it's all about *Looking in From the Outside!*

"Here is the test to find out if your mission on Earth is finished: if you're alive, it isn't."

- Richard Bach

Activity Two

Your Mode (M.O.D.E.)

There are hundreds of assessment tools available that measure a person's personality, preferences, tendencies, or skills. They are designed to help a person better understand themselves and other people around them. Some instruments are more complicated than others, but they are all still based on some model of psychology or philosophy and framed around an aspect of personality, physiology or behavior.

Some of the simpler tools available are divided into quadrants or four primary areas providing an easy way to gain a clearer picture of oneself in a reasonable amount of time. However, you still must complete an assessment and wait for the results. The most interesting thing about the process is that people tend to already know themselves well enough that they can predict where they will fit in the different categories. In fact, when a group of individuals attends a leadership seminar or professional training course requiring them to complete some instruments in advance, most of them can indicate with great accuracy the results of their profile before they are given their reports. So if this is the case, then why not just provide the different common categories describing types of behavior and let people choose which ones fit them best? Let's do just that.

In this exercise, you will be the expert about yourself. Why? Because you know more about yourself than anyone else does! This is not to say that others can't provide meaningful feedback (which will be discussed later in other exercises), but you are quite the expert in many ways. Take a look at the following four descriptions and rate yourself on each of the categories to decide which styles best describe who you are:

Which of these behavioral styles is most like you?

- ✓ The **M**ONITOR
- ✓ The **O**BSERVER
- ✓ The **D**ELEGATOR
- ✓ The **E**NERGIZER

Take a look at each of the following descriptions and rate yourself on a scale from 1 to 10, where 10 is very much like you and 1 is not like you at all. Place your score in the space provided above each style after you read the description.

MONITOR

Your Self Rating _____
(on a scale from 1 to 10)

You are a <u>Monitor</u> if you do these things:

- Tend to be detail-oriented
- Like to follow policies & procedures
- Strive for accuracy
- Like to check for mistakes
- Enjoy putting things in precise order
- Do not make quick decisions
- Like to check & double check for mistakes
- Recognize the littlest details
- Remind people of the rules

OBSERVER

Your Self Rating _____
(on a scale from 1 to 10)

You are an <u>Observer</u> if you do these things:

- Keep a steady pace in life
- Go with the flow
- Tend to avoid conflict of any kind
- Are not a major risk taker
- Appreciate consistency
- Are very loyal to a group
- Don't want to "rock the boat."
- Tend to keep to yourself
- Do more listening than talking

DELEGATOR

Your Self Rating _____
(on a scale from 1 to 10)

You are a **Delegator** if you do these things:

- Want quick results
- Like to delegate work to others
- Do not like too many details
- Like to take on challenges
- Tend to look at the "Big Picture"
- Enjoy managing others
- Do not like being managed
- Welcome conflict
- Can become impatient at times

ENERGIZER

Your Self Rating _____
(on a scale from 1 to 10)

You are an **Energizer** if you do these things:

- Are the "energy" of a group
- Like being involved
- Do not like lots of data or analyses
- Like being around people
- Get bored easily if not active
- Enjoy planning events
- Like being creative and expressive
- Tend to be talkative or outgoing
- Get excited about new plans

Now that you've rated yourself on each of the styles, provide your own results below. Place your ratings (1 to 10) next to each behavioral style:

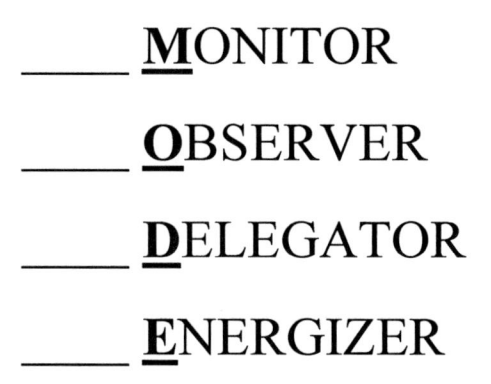

____ **M**ONITOR

____ **O**BSERVER

____ **D**ELEGATOR

____ **E**NERGIZER

Now plot these numbers to match each letter on the graph below and then connect the dots with a line:

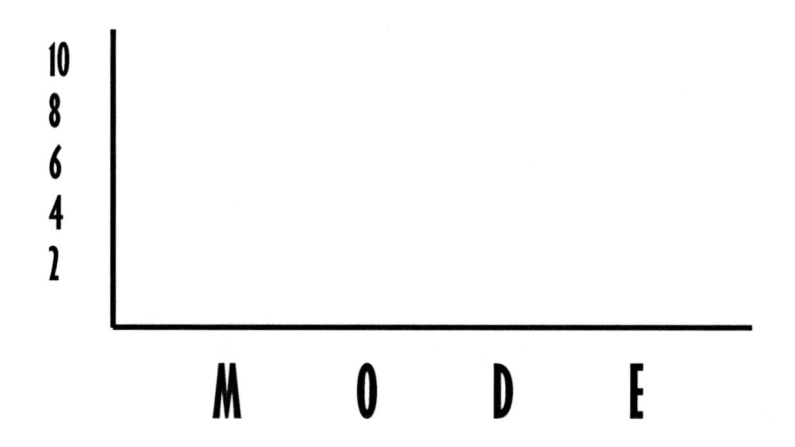

```
10
 8
 6
 4
 2
     M    O    D    E
```

Congratulations! You have just completed a personal behavioral style assessment by yourself. You didn't have to answer fifty questions, you didn't have to pay $150, and you didn't have to attend a training workshop to get your results. Now it's time to learn how to use these results, also known as the "So What?" factor.

It is important for you to know that these types of instruments are intended to do one thing; create a better understanding of yourself and those around you. As a result, these tools can help you enhance communication, improve interpersonal dynamics, and provide an opportunity to develop as an individual. It is therefore essential that you recognize your own characteristics and begin looking at the characteristics of other people more closely. So how do you do that? Let's practice.

Notice how you scored high on one or more of the styles and lower on other styles. (High is a rating of 5 or more than 5, and Low is a rating of 4 or less than 4). If you rate higher on one style as compared to the other styles then you are more likely to engage in those kinds of behaviors. If you rate lower on one or more styles, you are less likely to engage in those behaviors.

In order to practice using these findings, you will need to identify people you know who fit into each of the identified categories; Monitor, Observer, Delegator, and Energizer. Place a name beside each style on the next page of someone who would score high on that style. Use four different people in your life:

Fill in the names in the spaces below:

_____ is definitely a <u>MONITOR</u>

_____ is definitely an <u>OBSERVER</u>

_____ is definitely a <u>DELEGATOR</u>

_____ is definitely an <u>ENERGIZER</u>

Now answer the following questions to see an example of how this instrument can begin to help you improve your interactions and relationships with others, based on their own MODE. Use the spaces to fill in the same names you used above:

Questions

1. How might you best approach the high **MONITOR**, _____, if you work on a project or goal together?

2. How might you best approach the high **OBSERVER**, _____, if you work on a project or goal together?

3. How might you best approach the high **DELEGATOR**, _____, if you work on a project or goal together?

4. How might you best approach the high **ENERGIZER**, _____, if you work on a project or goal together?

Conclusion

You can begin to see how this simple approach can force you to think more deeply about others than you typically do. It takes a little more effort and a little more time, but that's how personal development works – it takes time and effort. The benefit of engaging in the activities in this book is that you won't have to spend too much time figuring out how to use these tools; instead you can get right to using them!

The M.O.D.E. assessment allows you to create a new vocabulary for you and groups or teams with whom you work or interact. The people in your team can identify which style(s) describe them accurately and then you can have a conversation about their needs, skills, tendencies, strengths, weaknesses etc. This will ensure that each person is more likely to be doing something they enjoy rather than being "stuck" doing something they dislike or hate doing! For example, a "high-level" ENERGIZER would likely be much more productive and engaged if s/he were involved in the planning of an event rather than being in charge of data analyses for a team, whereas a "high-level" MONITOR would likely enjoy analyzing data and preparing complex reports.

This simple instrument can also provide an opportunity for you to adjust from being in the ENERGIZER mode, for example, to being engaged in the OBSERVER mode when it is more appropriate, or help you decrease your tendency to be too engaged in the DELEGATOR mode and not using enough of the MONITOR mode at times. You can increase and decrease the levels of each of these modes as each situation changes. It just takes ongoing practice and increased self-awareness. Flexibility is the benefit of a behaviorally-based instrument like this. And another great thing about the MODE instrument is that you already know how you fit in the modes and how those around you fit in these modes. We sometimes rely too much on advice from others for answers that are right in front of us!

"Advice is what we ask for when we already know the answer but wish we didn't."

- Erica Jong

Activity Three

The Best Fit

The personal development industry offers many career planning tools to help you find a job that matches your interests and skills. Some of these tools are more complex than others, but each of them prompts you to look at how well your job and desires fit together. In keeping with the theme of simplicity, this next exercise will provide a very simple version of the instruments available, giving you instant results to determine if you are in the most appropriate occupation or field of work. This activity will also give you the opportunity to consider what changes if any you may want to make in your current role at work or your role outside of work.

Think about the important factors in your life inside and outside of work. Some of the factors are similar in both environments, but some may vary. For example, you may prefer to have a work environment that gives you plenty of time to concentrate on research or data, but have a life outside of work focused on interactions with others with a more socially-oriented focus. Conversely, you may be a person who likes work to look very much like your personal life. There are no correct or incorrect preferences; this is about what you want or need in your work and personal environments. Even if you're retired, this exercise can help you determine if you are in an environment that complements your desires and needs.

"Choose a job you love and you'll never work a day in your life."

— Confucius

On the next two pages, you will see two charts. In the first chart, fill in the boxes to the left with characteristics of a work setting that are attractive and/or important to you. Then check the box next to each of the characteristics noting if they do or don't exist in *your* current work environment.

In the second chart, fill in the boxes to the left with characteristics of a personal environment that are attractive and/or important to you. Then check the box next the characteristics noting if they do or don't exist in *your* personal life outside of your work environment.

Example:

Characteristics that are Attractive or Important to me in the Workplace	Does Exist	Doesn't Exist	Seldom Exists
High level of Creativity			X

WORK ENVIRONMENT

Characteristics that are Attractive or Important to me in the Workplace	Does Exist	Doesn't Exist	Seldom Exists

Example:

Characteristics that are Attractive or Important to me Outside of Work	Does Exist	Doesn't Exist	Seldom Exists
Chance to Relax Alone	X		

PERSONAL ENVIRONMENT

Characteristics that are Attractive or Important to me Outside of Work	Does Exist	Doesn't Exist	Seldom Exists

Questions

Answer the following questions in the space provided:

1. How well are the characteristics you listed being met in your current <u>work environment</u>, why or why not?

2. How well are the characteristics you listed being met in your current <u>personal environment</u>, why or why not?

3. How similar / different are your work and personal environments? How does that affect your level of overall satisfaction in life?

4. What would you <u>change</u> and what would you <u>keep</u> in your work or personal environments to create the best fit for you?

Conclusion

While this activity is a simple version of some of the more complex vocational development tools, never underestimate the complex nature of simplicity! Use the results of this exercise to develop your own plan for improving your current and future work and personal environments. As you continue to complete the activities that follow, also keep in mind that you will be combining all of this information in a final personal development plan at the end of this workbook.

Activity Four

360 Degree Assessment

Some people are familiar with a traditional 360 Degree Assessment, while others may have never heard of this tool. Not unlike the other activities and instruments completed in previous sections, the 360 Degree Assessment in this exercise provides a very simple, easy-to-use version. Whether you have completed many 360's or are new to the instrument, you can benefit from this quick and purposeful version. First, to better understand the 360 Degree Assessment, you should know how and why it is designed.

While there are hundreds if not thousands of versions of this feedback instrument, the concept is basically the same: You ask people in your work-group, team setting, or any group environment to give you feedback about you. The feedback is provided from your bosses, coaches, instructors or mentors, and your peers, teammates or colleagues and your staff or those who support you, like administrative staff or mentees. The 360 feedback essentially comes from people all around you like a 360 degree circle, as the following diagram demonstrates, hence the term, *360 Degree Assessment*:

360 Degree Assessment

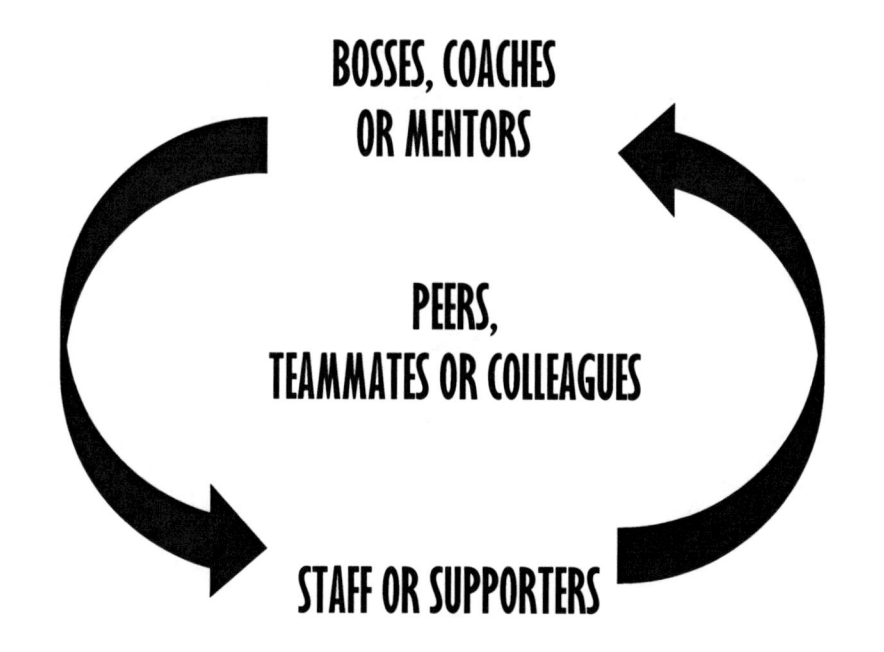

BOSSES, COACHES OR MENTORS

PEERS, TEAMMATES OR COLLEAGUES

STAFF OR SUPPORTERS

In order to gain feedback from each of these groups of people, you need to choose meaningful questions. Some of the most complex 360 Degree Assessments may ask 30 to 60 questions and have a preferred and actual score for each question, providing a gap analysis and statistical levels of significance. Those results are typically very useful, but require extra time to process and interpret. The following format provides a much simpler way to set up your very own 360 Degree Assessment right away with quick and easy-to-read results:

Use the following three stop, start, and continue questions to design your 360 Degree Assessment tool:

1. What should I <u>stop</u> doing that would help me become a more effective team member?

2. What should I <u>start</u> doing that would help me become a more effective team member?

3. What should I <u>continue</u> doing that would help me become a more effective team member?

Begin by answering these questions on your own:

SELF ASSESSMENT

1. What should I <u>stop</u> doing that would help me become a more effective team member?

2. What should I <u>start</u> doing that would help me become a more effective team member?

3. What should I <u>continue</u> doing that would help me become a more effective team member?

Next, make copies of the following sheets and hand them out to any of the people who fit in the Boss/Coach/Mentor, the Peer/Colleague/Teammate, and the Staff/Supporter 360 categories. Then ask them to complete and return these sheets in a confidential envelope or in some other confidential fashion, such as a suggestion box or other approach. Remember that you are the person being assessed, so your name should be in that space. There is no need for them to put their name on the sheet; it is more important that you receive the *feedback* rather than being concerned with who said what. If you do approach this task according to these rules, you are more likely to gain honest feedback and less resistance from your group.

You may also choose to re-type your own sheets and customize some questions that are more specifically related to your role. You may also decide to send this out electronically and combine the feedback in a spreadsheet or other creative format. The possibilities are endless.

BOSS OR COACH OR MENTOR ASSESSMENT

Please answer the following questions about this person:

Name of person being assessed: _____

1. What should I <u>stop</u> doing that would help me become a more effective team member?

2. What should I <u>start</u> doing that would help me become a more effective team member?

3. What should I <u>continue</u> doing that would help me become a more effective team member?

PEER OR COLLEAGUE OR TEAMMATE ASSESSMENT

Please answer the following questions about this person:

Name of person being assessed: _____

1. What should I <u>stop</u> doing that would help me become a more effective team member?

2. What should I <u>start</u> doing that would help me become a more effective team member?

3. What should I <u>continue</u> doing that would help me become a more effective team member?

STAFF OR SUPPORTER ASSESSMENT

Please answer the following questions about this person:

Name of person being assessed: _____

1. What should I <u>stop</u> doing that would help me become a more effective team member?

2. What should I <u>start</u> doing that would help me become a more effective team member?

3. What should I <u>continue</u> doing that would help me become a more effective team member?

Conclusion

While this is a very simplified version of a traditional 360 Degree Assessment, you may find it extremely valuable. For example, you will use this feedback as part of your personal development plan. You can also choose to engage in some meaningful conversations with your team about their responses, which will help you to better understand their expectations of you. Remember to always keep an open mind and be as non-defensive as possible when examining your team's responses. Feedback is one of the most valuable gifts you can receive from someone, even if it can sometimes be difficult to hear.

"Always keep an open mind.
An open mind is a good thing.
But don't keep your mind
so open that your brains fall out."

- Maharani of Jaipur

Activity Five

People You Know

How well we know the people around us *does* matter. It affects how we interact with them, the assumptions we make about them and the quality of communication we experience with each other. This next activity will help you identify how well you know the people in your life and guide you through ways to use that valuable information. As mentioned previously, the results of these activities will be used together, helping you form your own personal development plan at the end of this workbook. In this activity, you will already be asked to combine your knowledge from the MODE instrument you completed in Activity Two.

Using the following empty pie charts, place the name of individuals you know from any particular environment, whether it be school, work, home or any other setting. Then place a letter from the MODE activity in the provided space next to their name that describes which mode they most likely resemble. Finally, fill in pieces of their pie based on how well you know them.

> "Self knowledge comes from knowing others."
>
> - J.W. von Goethe

Example:

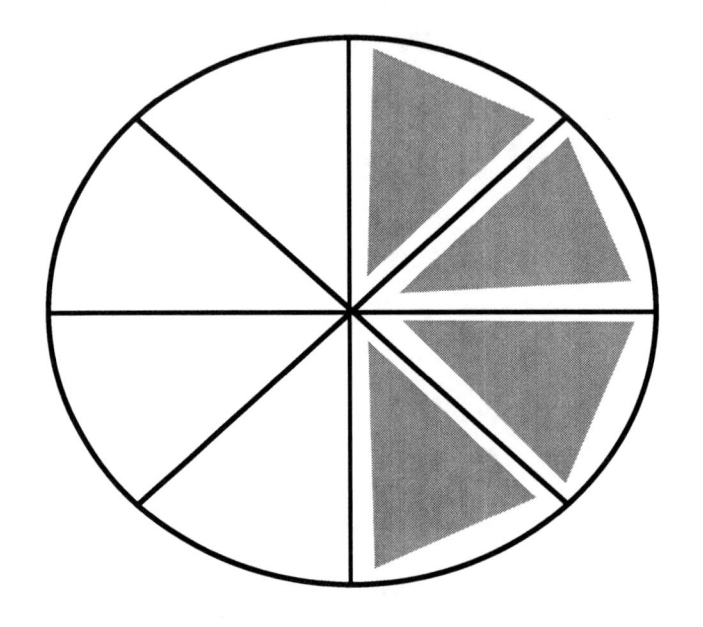

Name: _John Smith_   **Mode:** _O_

In the example above, I know John fairly well, so I fill in four slices. I also know that he tends to keep to himself and be more of an Observer, rather than a Monitor, Delegator, or Energizer, so I place an "O" indicating his most dominant mode.

Now do the same thing with any group of people you want to use. They may all be part of an intact group with which you belong or they can be people from a variety of settings in your life. It's up to you to determine how the group is organized.

Use the next page to write in the names and modes of each person in the grouping you've chosen. Also fill in the number of slices according to how well you know each person. Then answer the questions on the page that follows.

People You Know

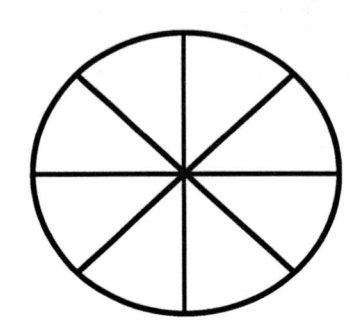

Name: _____ Mode: 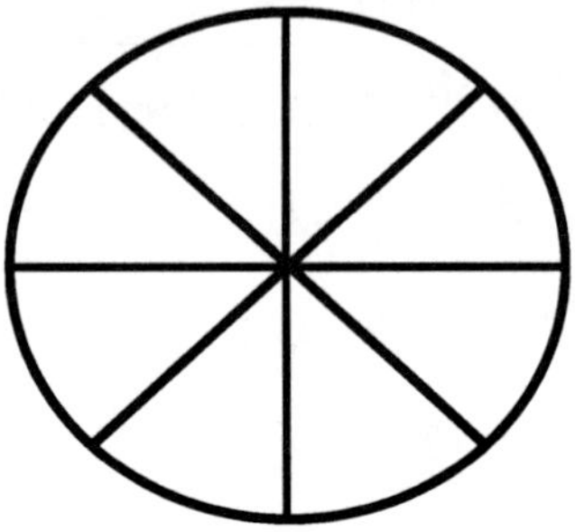 ___   Name: _____ Mode: ___

Name: _____ Mode:  ___   Name: _____ Mode: ___

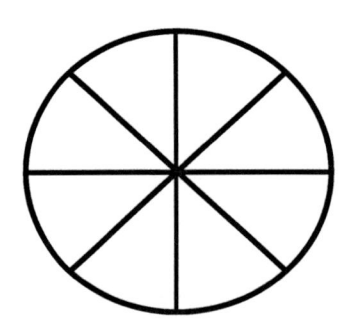

Name: _____ Mode: 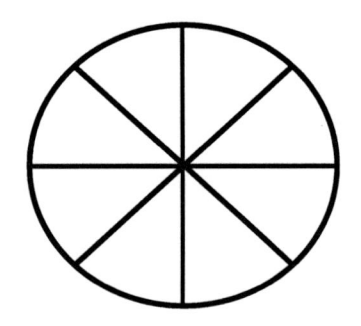 ___   Name: _____ Mode: ___

Questions

Answer the following questions in the spaces below:

1. Who do you know very well and why?

2. Who do you <u>not</u> know very well and why not?

3. How does knowing someone well help you? How does it challenge you?

4. How does <u>not</u> knowing someone well help you? How does it challenge you?

5. What do you find interesting about the pie chart results and why?

Conclusion

While this may seem like a simple process, once you begin doing this naturally in your daily environments, you can begin to see how valuable this process is. You can actually use this method with a larger group and have conversations about what these differences and similarities mean to the organization or team.

The activities thus far have been designed to have you think about your present and familiar life settings. In the next activity, you'll have the chance to stretch yourself and explore unfamiliar territory.

Activity Six

Mental Stretching

As a result of regularly stretching our muscles, we become more flexible. Just as we can stretch our muscles, so can we stretch our minds. When we stretch our bodies, we become more able to move in ways we otherwise would not be capable of without injuring ourselves. Similarly, if we develop conclusions without first exercising our minds, we can easily injure our thinking or make incorrect assumptions.

This next development activity will help challenge you to stretch your mind so that you may better understand the world and people around you! If you think you've seen most everything, you may be surprised. If you recognize that there is plenty left for you to see and learn, then you are already prepared for this next exercise.

As a result of completing this activity, you should be better able to recognize some of the assumptions you make about your surroundings and how that can affect your beliefs and actions. The more you push yourself in this experience, the greater the rewards or insights you will achieve.

"All growth is a leap in the dark, a spontaneous unpremeditated act without benefit of experience."

– Henry Miller

Take a moment to describe four different settings or situations with which you are familiar:

Example:

a. *Eating lunch with a friend or co-worker*

1. _____

2. _____

3. _____

4. _____

After completing this list, begin to think about a few settings that aren't so familiar to you. Read the examples of settings that may not be familiar to most people that are listed on the following page:

Mental Stretching Examples:

1. Factory
2. Retirement Center
3. Manufacturing Plant
4. Ride-along with a law enforcement officer
5. Cultural parade different from your own culture
6. Military base or military hospital
7. Religious or cultural center other than yours
8. All male or all female organizational meeting

Your challenge is to choose one setting that would be a stretch for you to attend or observe. You must choose something that is not familiar and may actually seem somewhat uncomfortable or a challenge for you to attend. List several ideas on the next page that you may consider to be your own mental stretching projects.

Mental Stretching Settings to Consider:

1. _____

2. _____

3. _____

4. _____

5. _____

In order to complete this activity, you must attend one of these settings or events listed above and write about the experience. You should use the Writing Panels on the following pages. Provide as much detail about the experience as you can (for example: who you met, what you learned, etc.). Finally, after writing about your experience, you will then be asked to answer the questions at the end of this chapter.

Mental Stretching Writing Panel One

Mental Stretching Writing Panel Two

Mental Stretching Writing Panel Three

Questions

Answer the following questions in the space provided:

1. What was the most challenging part of the mental stretching experience and why?

2. What surprised you most about the experience?

3. What was the most enjoyable part, if any, of the exercise and why?

4. Would you choose the same experience again, why or why not?

Conclusion

Mental Stretching is a powerful exercise that can help you expand your mind. If you engage in this process regularly, you will continue to build a more comprehensive understanding of the world around you. It is easy to find ourselves in a routine where we never get a chance to experience something new. We either put it off for another day or we just don't realize there is something else out there for us to explore. If you found meaning or purpose in this exercise, challenge yourself to do it again. Choose a different setting this time and answer the same questions as a way to better understand the experience. Challenge other people in your life to do the same.

Activity Seven

Personal Development Plan

Teams, organizations, education institutions and corporations utilize personal development plans as a way to foster individual growth. This emphasis on self-awareness has become more common due to emerging evidence that clearly demonstrates the positive effects of self-development, self-reflection or self-exploration. These positive effects include higher levels of productivity, increased likelihood of engagement in the workplace, a greater ability to interact with others and a clearer understanding of one's role in a team or organization.

In this final activity, you will put together your own PDP. This is your opportunity to combine all the activities in this workbook resulting in a personal action plan, also known as a Personal Development Plan (PDP). Take the time to make this plan as thorough and meaningful as you can. Be honest with yourself, be realistic, but don't limit your plan; Stretch, Focus, and Believe!

Your PDP will be made up of six parts, like the panels of a window:

My Life Story	Your M.O.D.E.
The Best Fit	360 Degrees
People You Know	Mental Stretching

Personal Development Plan

Name: _____

Date: _____

Part One: My Life Story

1. Choose an area from your Life Story that especially relates to your development and explain here:

2. What is a goal you want to set related to that personal development area?

3. What actions are necessary to achieve that goal?

4. How will you know you've achieved that goal?

Part Two: Your MODE

1. What is your highest MODE?

2. Explain how you plan to interact with the other MODEs:

   Monitors:

   Observers:

   Delegators:

   Energizers:

3. How can you further utilize the MODE assessment tool in your organization?

Part Three: The Best Fit

1. How well does your current job match your interests?

2. If it is a poor match, how might you change your role? If it is a good match, how will you maintain that?

3. What specific areas of your work or personal life do you want to focus on; what's most important to you?

4. Are there other thoughts or ideas you have that will result in a best fit between your desires and both your personal and work settings?

Part Four: 360 Degrees

1. How can you use this 360 Degree Assessment in your organization? How might you design your own?

2. What are some ways you can engage your team in this process, how will you discuss feedback?

3. What specific actions must you take in order to implement this process?

4. Are there other ideas you have based on this process?

Part Five: People You Know

1. Do you see value in reflecting on how well you know people around you? Why or why not?

2. Who do you think you need to know more about and why?

3. How will you go about getting to know someone better?

4. Using the charts below, complete two descriptions of people you want to get to know better and think about how you might engage them, based on your descriptions:

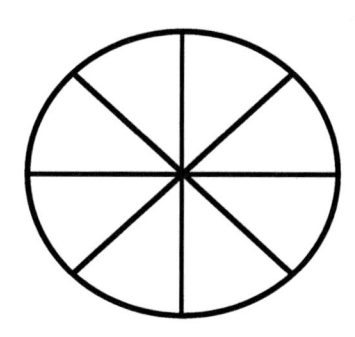

Name: _____   Name: _____
Mode: _____   Mode: _____

Part Six: Mental Stretching

1. What was the most valuable part of the Mental Stretching exercise for you?

2. List several Mental Stretching events you will consider completing in the future:

   _____
   _____
   _____
   _____
   _____

3. How often do you plan to engage in Mental Stretching?

4. What do you hope to gain from Mental Stretching in your own personal development?

Don't forget to complete the following Post-Test:

Rate the following statements according to the 5-point scale below. Circle the most appropriate number below each statement.

1 = Strongly Disagree

2 = Disagree

3 = Neither Agree nor Disagree

4 = Agree

5 = Strongly Agree

1. I clearly understand myself.
   1   2   3   4   5

2. I clearly understand the people around me.
   1   2   3   4   5

3. I clearly understand why I behave the way I do.
   1   2   3   4   5

4. I clearly understand how my behavior affects other people.
   1   2   3   4   5

5. I clearly understand the needs of other people.
   1   2   3   4   5

6. I clearly understand how people perceive me.
   1   2   3   4   5

"What is necessary to change
a person is to change
their awareness of themselves."

- Abraham Maslow

Final Thoughts

Based on the similar or different scores from your Pre-Test to your Post-Test, ask yourself why you may have responded the way that you did. There are no right or wrong answers. Instead it is important for you to consider how your perceptions of yourself may have changed or remained the same following the tasks you've completed in this personal development workbook.

You are encouraged to use this workbook as a development tool in your organization. In doing so, you will increase open dialogue, promote self-development, and most importantly have a chance to work through some of the challenges we all face in our own personal and organizational settings.

Too often, we go through life with some sort of blinders on. The challenge this workbook puts forth is to look at life from a perspective that we seldom do -- a perspective from the outside. Bill Nelson was fortunate to have a life-changing experience while he was gazing through a US Space Shuttle window. It is the intention of this personal development workbook to help *you* create *your* own window.

Please visit our website:

www.telic.org

... where you'll find more exciting resources for your own development and the development of your organization!

Personal Notes

Personal Notes

Personal Notes

Personal Notes

Personal Notes

Personal Notes

Personal Notes

Personal Notes

Personal Notes

Personal Notes

Personal Notes

Personal Notes

Please visit our website:

www.telic.org

...where you'll find more exciting resources for your own development and the development of your organization!

LaVergne, TN USA
07 February 2011
215646LV00007B/27/P